the prin

G000020289

pres

JUDGEMENT
DAY

a new version of Ibsen's *When We Dead Awaken*
by Mike Poulton

Judgement Day was first produced at The Print Room
on 16 November 2011

JUDGEMENT DAY

a new version of Ibsen's *When We Dead Awaken*
by Mike Poulton

Arnold Rubek	Michael Pennington
Maia	Sara Vickers
A Hotel Manager	Peter Symonds
Baron Ulfheim	Philip Correia
Lars	Andrew Hanratty
Irena de Satoff	Penny Downie
A Nun	Jane Thorne
Director	James Dacre
Designer	Mike Britton
Composer/Sound Designer	Richard Hammarton
Casting Director	Anji Carroll
Assistant Director	Will Wrightson
Production Manager	Alex Stone
Stage Manager	Hannah Gore
Technical Stage Manager	Brian Perkins
Production Photographer	Sheila Burnett

For The Print Room

Artistic Directors	Anda Winters & Lucy Bailey
Producer	Veronica Humphris
Line Producer	Emily Vaughan-Barratt
Production Assistant	Fenella Dawnay
Literary Coordinator	Zena Birch
FOH Manager	Margaret Clunie
Master Carpenter	Rodger Pampilo
Press Representative	Mobius Industries
Production Sound Services	Gauge Productions

With special thanks to: Izzy Brain, Dr Cindy Lawford,
Emma McKie, Edox Westbourne Grove, Philip O'Donnell

Introduction

When We Dead Awaken was Ibsen's final play before a series of crippling strokes silenced him. It's a play for grown-ups. It is rarely performed – often considered difficult, even, at times, impenetrable. Its symbolism is, on first reading, not easy to fathom. Yet – even on first reading – it has the power to cast the same sort of spell as his youthful, mystical verse dramas *Peer Gynt* and *Brand*. Or that was my feeling when I first began to struggle with it many, many years ago. Part of its attraction for me has been the play's mysteries – the challenge of unlocking its secrets – trying to offer access to them – without reducing them by trying to over-explain them. In the original, Ibsen casts himself as an artist, talking to other artists about the constraints everyday, human needs place upon genius. He offers a lifetime's experience as one of the most original thinkers of his day on the necessary coupling of brilliant technique and inspiration. He speaks autobiographically about how and why women affected his development as an artist. He is astute, he is profound, and he is, at times – as Ibsen always is – very funny. For me, *Judgement Day*, as I have called it, is Ibsen's last confession – his last word, or even his last judgement on his life as a playwright. It's a brilliant swansong.

Mike Poulton

Cast and Company Biographies

Philip Correia – *Baron Ulfheim*
Theatre includes: *The Syndicate, Hobson's Choice* (Chichester/tour); *The History Boys* (National Theatre/Wyndham's/tour); *Bus Stop* (New Vic/Stephen Joseph, Scarborough); *The Cherry Orchard* (Birmingham Rep); *Country Music* (West Yorkshire Playhouse); *Northern Odyssey* (Live Theatre, Newcastle); *What Cheryl Did Next* (Theatre503); *Romeo and Juliet* (Jermyn Street); *The Merry Wives of Windsor* (RSC).

Television includes: *Vera, Hollyoaks, Canoe Man, Lewis, Casualty, Doctors, The Bill.*

Film includes: *The Hunters, Matchmaker.*

Philip trained at LAMDA.

Penny Downie – *Irena de Satoff*
Theatre includes: *The Merchant of Venice* (Globe Classic Best Actress Award), *Hamlet* (RSC); *Henry V, Dinner* (National Theatre); *Helen* (Shakespeare's Globe); *An Ideal Husband* (West End/Broadway).

Television includes: *The Shadowline, Waking the Dead, Law and Order, Silk, New Tricks, Poirot, Byron, New Street Law, The Cazalets, The Ice House.*

Film includes: *Invictus, W.E., The Girl on the Bicycle, House of Mirth, Food of Love, Crime and Punishment, Wetherby, Crosstalk, Round the Bend.*

Penny is an Associate Artist of the Royal Shakespeare Company.

Andrew Hanratty – *Lars*
Theatre includes: *Orpheus and Eurydice* (Old Vic Tunnels/National Youth Theatre); *It's a Scandal* (Etcetera).

Film includes: *Scarcely Here.*

Andrew has recently graduated from Drama Studio London.

Michael Pennington – *Arnold Rubek*
Theatre includes : Ibsen's *John Gabriel Borkman* (ETT); and *The Master Builder* (Chichester); *Hamlet, Timon of Athens* (RSC); *Collaboration, Taking Sides* (Duchess); *Sweet William, Anton Chekhov* (solo shows); *The Wars of the Roses* (English Shakespeare Company).

Television includes: *Trial and Retribution, State of Play, Kavanagh QC.*

Film includes: *Churchill at War, The Iron Lady.*

He is also a director and writer and was Joint Artistic Director of the English Shakespeare Company.

Peter Symonds – *A Hotel Manager*
Theatre includes: *Black 'Ell* (Soho); *Forgotten Voices* (Pleasance); *Anthony and Cleopatra*, *Caesar and Cleopatra* (Clwyd Theatr Cymru); *Kafka's Dick* (Leeds); *Othello* (Bristol Old Vic); *Bedroom Farce* (National Theatre); *Outward Bound* (Yvonne Arnaud); *Habeus Corpus*, *Conduct Unbecoming*, *Outside Edge* (national tours).

Television includes: *Doctor Who*, *Garrow's Law*, *Sharpe's Challenge*, *Miss Marple*, *Lewis*, *EastEnders*, *The Long Firm*, *55 Degrees North*, *Who Gets the Dog?*, *The Final Cut*, *The Guilty*, *The Big Battalions*, *The Darling Buds of May*.

Film includes: *The Lawless Heart*, *Project Gotha*, *Waiting for Exit Music*, *Labyrinth*, *The Keeper*, *Callan*, *The Gift*, *Dreams*, *John and Yoko*, *Out on a Limb*.

Sara Vickers – *Maia*
Theatre includes: *'Tis Pity She's a Whore* (West Yorkshire Playhouse); *The Lady from the Sea* (Manchester Royal Exchange); *Measure for Measure* (RADA).

Television includes: *Bert & Dickie*.

Sara trained at RADA.

Mike Poulton – Writer
Mike Poulton began writing for the theatre in 1995. His first two productions were staged the following year at the Chichester Festival Theatre: *Uncle Vanya* and *Fortune's Fool*. Since then, productions include Schiller's *Wallenstein* (Chichester Festival Theatre); *Mary Stuart*, Terry Hands' *The Cherry Orchard* (Clwyd Theatre Cymru); *The Lady from the Sea* (Birmingham Rep); *The Canterbury Tales* (RSC); *The Father* (Chichester Minerva Theatre); and *Uncle Vanya* on Broadway. Earlier productions include *The Dance of Death*, Euripides' *Ion* (Mercury Theatre Colchester); *Ghosts* (Plymouth Theatre Royal); *St Erkenwald* (RSC); and *Three Sisters* (Birmingham Rep).

In 2003 his *Fortune's Fool* on Broadway received a Tony nomination for Best Play and went on to win seven major awards including the Tony for Best Actor for Alan Bates, and the Tony for Best Featured Actor for Frank Langella. In 2005, his adaptation of Schiller's *Don Carlos* (Crucible, Sheffield and West End) won an Olivier Award.

He was commissioned by Horipro to write *Anjin (The English Samurai)* which opened in 2009 in Tokyo, followed by a season in Osaka. In 2010, his dramatisation of Malory's *Morte d'Arthur* opened at the Courtyard Theatre in Stratford-upon-Avon and his adaptation of *The Bacchae* was produced at Manchester's Royal Exchange.

This year, his new version of Schiller's *Luise Miller* had a summer season at the Donmar and the premiere of *The Syndicate*, a translation of Eduardo De Filippo's *Il Sindaco del Rione Sanità* opened at Chichester, followed by a UK tour.

James Dacre – Director

James's Dacre's directing credits include *King James Bible* (National Theatre); *As You Like It* (Shakespeare's Globe/European tour); *Orpheus and Eurydice* (Old Vic Tunnels/National Youth Theatre); *The Unconquered* (Stellar Quines/UK tour/Off-Broadway transfer); and *Desire Under the Elms*, *Copenhagen* and *Bus Stop* at the New Vic Theatre, where he was Artistic Associate. His world premiere production of *The Mountaintop* (Theatre503 and Trafalgar Studios) won the 2010 Olivier Award for Best New Play and was nominated for a further five awards, and *Precious Little Talent* (Trafalgar Studios) won Best Play at the 2011 London Theatre Festival Awards, and has been nominated for an Evening Standard Award. James has directed world premieres by Suzan Lori Parks, Torben Betts, Lucy Thurber, Ella Hickson, Katori Hall, Dic Edwards, Ed Kemp and Molly Davies, amongst others. He has been awarded Fulbright and Schubert Fellowships in Theatre Directing and trained on the ITV/Channel 4 Regional Theatre Director's Scheme.

Mike Britton – Designer

Previously at The Print Room: *Fabrication.*

Theatre includes: *Broken Glass* (West End/Tricycle); *Much Ado About Nothing* (Shakespeare's Globe); '*Tis Pity She's a Whore, Hay Fever, Dial M For Murder* (West Yorkshire Playhouse); *The Deep Blue Sea/Rattigan's Nijinsky* (Chichester); *Statement of Regret* (National Theatre); *Faith Healer* (Bristol Old Vic Studio); *The Winter's Tale, Pericles, Madness in Valencia* (RSC); *The Vertical Hour* (Royal Court); *That Face* (Royal Court/West End); *The Late Middle Classes* (Donmar Warehouse); *Period of Adjustment* (Almeida); *Nakamitsu* (Gate); *Glass Eels, Comfort Me With Apples* (Hampstead); *The Tales Of Ballycumber, The Three Sisters* (Abbey, Dublin); *Henry V* (Manchester Evening Post Award for Best Design); *Mirandolina* (Manchester Royal Exchange); *Wuthering Heights, The Lady from the Sea* (TMA Award for Best Design), *She Stoops to Conquer* (Birmingham Rep); *Les Liaisons Dangereuses, Arsenic and Old Lace, People at Sea* (Salisbury Playhouse); *Noises Off, Dr Faustus* (Liverpool Playhouse); *Don't Look Now* (Lyceum Sheffield/Lyric Hammersmith); *The Comedy of Errors, Bird Calls* (Crucible, Sheffield); *Rudolf* (Raimund Theatre, Vienna).

Richard Hammarton – Composer/Sound Designer

Theatre Composition and Sound Design credits include: *Dr Faustus, Edward ll* (Manchester Royal Exchange); *Speaking in Tongues, Ghosts* (West End); *The Mountaintop* (Trafalgar Studios/Theatre503); *The Rise and Fall of Little Voice* (Harrogate); *Six Characters in Search of an Author, A Raisin in the Sun* (Young Vic); *Dealer's Choice, The Shooky* (Birmingham Rep); *Pride and Prejudice* (Bath Theatre Royal/UK tour); *Some Kind of Bliss, Hello and Goodbye* (Trafalgar Studios); *People at Sea, Les Liasions Dangereuses, The Real Thing, The Constant Wife, Arsenic and Old Lace, Persuasion* (Salisbury Playhouse).

Television Composition credits include: *Agatha Christie's Marple*, *Wipeout*, *Sex 'n' Death*.

Television/Film Orchestration credits include: *Primeval*, *Jericho*, *If I Had You*, *Take Me*, *Dracula*, *Silent Witness*, *The Ship*, *Scenes of a Sexual Nature*, *The Nine Lives of Tomas Katz*.

Anji Carroll – Casting Director
Previously with James Dacre: *Precious Little Talent* (Trafalgar Studios); *Bus Stop*, *Desire Under the Elms*, *Copenhagen* (New Vic).

Theatre includes: *The Admirable Crichton*, *Spring and Port Wine*, *Proof*, *The Rivals*, *Peter Pan*, *Dumb Show*, *Honeymoon Suite* (New Vic); *Othello*, *Richard III* (Ludlow Festival); *The Ladykillers*, *Twelfth Night*, *The Deep Blue Sea*, *Macbeth*, *Notebook of Trigorin* (Northcott Theatre); *The Wizard of Oz*, *Who's Afraid Of Virginia Woolf?*, *Antigone*, *The Beggar's Opera*, *Chorus of Disapproval*, *Henry IV, Parts One* and *Two*, *Wind in the Willows* and *Betrayal* (Bristol Old Vic).

Television includes: *Titanic: Flesh & Steel Vs Nature*, *The Cup*, *The Bill*, *The Sarah Jane Adventures*, two series of *London's Burning* and *The Knock*.

Film includes: *Papadopoulos & Sons*, *West Is West*, *Mrs Ratcliffe's Revolution*, *Out of Depth* and *The Jolly Boys' Last Stand*.

Radio includes: BBC 4's political drama series *Number Ten*.

Will Wrightson – Assistant Director
Theatre includes: (as Director) *Sonderkommando* (rehearsed reading, HighTide Festival); *The Magic Flute* (Opera Integra); *Mouth/Wash* (rehearsed reading, Young Vic); *Keats by Candlelight* (Sir John Soane Museum).

Other credits include: *Midnight Your Time* (Assistant Director, HighTide Festival and Edinburgh); *Precious Little Talent* (Assistant Director, Trafalgar Studios); *Lingua Franca* (Associate Director and Producer, Finborough Theatre and 59E59 Theaters, New York); *Threshold* (Producer, Edinburgh Fringe Festival, Total Theatre Award nomination); *The Old Man and the Sea* (Producer, Brighton Fringe Festival, Argus Angel Award).

Will is Resident Assistant Director at HighTide Festival Theatre.

the print room

'If this kind of difficult, classy work is what we are to expect from the newly opened Print Room, artistic directors Lucy Bailey and Anda Winters are poised to make some real waves with this powerful new venue' *What's On Stage,* 2010

'The Print Room has fast become one of the most exciting fringe venues in London, and the finished product reaffirms what I've long suspected about The Print Room: that every production it programs turns into a must-see' *The Spectator,* 2011

Ibsen's *Judgement Day* continues The Print Room's policy of unearthing little-known works by major playwrights. It is one of Ibsen's least performed plays and has not been seen professionally in London for at least seventeen years. Lucy Bailey's collaboration with Mike Poulton began five years ago when she directed his version of *The Lady from the Sea.* Mike Poulton is one of our foremost interpreters of Ibsen and it is an honour to be given the opportunity to stage the world premier of his new version of *Judgement Day.*

History

The Print Room was founded in 2008 by Anda Winters and Lucy Bailey. After three years of renovation, the venue was officially opened in 2010 with a four-day exhibition of work **The Imaginary Painters Workshop** by Belgian artists Sofie Lachaert and Luc D'Hanis. This was followed by the UK premiere of the verse drama **Fabrication** by Pier Paolo Pasolini. Their first winter season culminated with **The City of Lost Angels**, a theatrical staging of the new album *Notes on Death* by the singer Petra Jean Phillipson.

In 2011, two more rare theatrical works by well-known writers were staged to great critical acclaim: the London premiere of the comedy thriller **Snake in the Grass** by Alan Ayckbourn, and a timely revival of **Kingdom of Earth** by Tennessee Williams, to coincide with the writer's centenary year.

They ended the first summer season with a two-week festival of multidisciplinary work by The Print Room's very own emerging artists scheme, **The Devils Festival**, and a series of **Summer Concerts** by international artists.

This was followed in September by The Print Room's first ever co-production, working alongside the Young Vic to present a rare double bill of Pinter plays: **One for the Road** and **Victoria Station.**

The Print Room is delighted to have been nominated this year for The Peter Brook Empty Space Award.

The Print Room is kindly supported by: Kate & Tony Best, BlueMountain Capital Management, David Crook, Mimi Gilligan, Mr & Mrs Michotte, The Nasr Family, Studio Indigo (Architects and Interior Designers) and Vehiria Veidet-Janbon.

The Print Room is a registered charity no: 1141921

www.the-print-room.org

JUDGEMENT DAY

Mike Poulton

Adapted from Henrik Ibsen's
WHEN WE DEAD AWAKEN

Characters

ARNOLD RUBEK, *a rich and successful sculptor*
MAIA, *his young wife*
A HOTEL MANAGER
BARON ULFHEIM, *a hunter*
LARS, *his valet and dog handler* (*non-speaking*)
IRENA DE SATOFF, *a rich guest at the hotel*
A NUN, *her companion*

This text went to press before the end of rehearsals and so may differ slightly from the play as performed.

ACT ONE

The terrace of a health spa. A sunny summer morning. There is a view of the fjord, and the sea beyond. Breakfast is over and PROFESSOR RUBEK *and* MAIA *are drinking champagne, and looking at the newspapers.* RUBEK *wears white summer, linen clothes, except for a black velvet jacket.* MAIA *is expensively and fashionably dressed.*

MAIA *sighs – almost unnoticeable.*

RUBEK. Hmm?

MAIA. Listen.

RUBEK. You feel it?

MAIA. What?

RUBEK. That silence.

MAIA *nods.*

Few people can.

MAIA. It's oppressive. Like before thunder.

RUBEK. Hmmm.

MAIA. Dead sound. Everywhere.

RUBEK. Ah… You'd rather not have come.

MAIA. Well.

RUBEK *won't answer.*

Surely you're not happy here?

RUBEK. Happy?

MAIA (*laughs*). How could I ask?

RUBEK. The sense of 'home' seems to have leaked out of the word 'country'… I've been away. Oh, I've been away.

MAIA. Go away again. (*Pause.*) Now. Let's go now.

RUBEK. Well…

MAIA. Back to the new house.

RUBEK (*smiles*). Home.

MAIA. House.

> RUBEK *smiles at her and shakes his head, perplexed.*

> Say –

RUBEK. Nothing.

MAIA. Yes.

> *Slight pause.*

RUBEK. It was not my choice –

MAIA. No.

RUBEK. Certainly couldn't have been mine.

MAIA. Everything's so… changed. And only four years since I left.

RUBEK. Four years since we married.

> MAIA *looks at the ground.*

> We have the villa on Lake Taunitz – a house in Rome – spacious – nothing to complain of – all that empty space… We don't bump into each other very often.

MAIA. Our lives are crammed full of space.

RUBEK. You've come up in the world. You were, let's face it, quite low.

MAIA. You think you've changed me?

RUBEK. I know I have.

MAIA. Hmm.

RUBEK. Change without progress.

MAIA. Nowhere to go.

RUBEK. I wonder if people ever change? Not the way they live… It reminds me of… (*Gives up.*)

MAIA. What does it remind you of?

RUBEK. Last night on the train.

MAIA. You slept all the way.

RUBEK. I did not sleep. I took in the silence – at all the little stations. Listening. Listening.

MAIA. Really?

RUBEK. Crossing the border – I knew I was home because the train began to stop at every station. Every tiny station. It was as if its sole purpose was to stop. And nothing happened.

MAIA. So why stop?

RUBEK. Nobody gets on or off. We're waiting, for hours, in a machine designed for motion – there's an overpowering intensity in the weight of a train's stillness – and there are two pointless men with a lantern walking up and down the track in the pitch darkness… mumbling things that have no meaning – thinking thoughts that are of no consequence…

MAIA. Always two of them. They have flat voices and they won't stop talking –

RUBEK. – about absolutely nothing. (*Pause*.) We'll get the steamer tomorrow – up to the Arctic.

MAIA. You won't find anybody there. No country – nothing to look at.

RUBEK. It isn't…

MAIA. Really?

RUBEK. Perhaps.

MAIA. If it's what you feel you need –

RUBEK. I don't *need* anything. There's nothing wrong with me.

MAIA. Oh, I think there is.

RUBEK. What?

MAIA. Why do you hate everybody? You're like a copper boiler with a broken valve – getting hotter and hotter and there's no release for the steam – and the pressure builds and builds and –

RUBEK. Shut your… (*Stops*.)

MAIA. And now you've come to hate your work.

Pause.

RUBEK. Have I?

MAIA. When we first met there were not enough hours in the day.

RUBEK. Times change.

MAIA. They certainly do. After you finished the great... (*Slight sneer.*)

RUBEK. I've no wish to discuss it. Not with you.

MAIA. Everybody says it's your masterpiece.

RUBEK. Then it must be. It must be, it must be, it must be –

MAIA. Everybody says it is –

RUBEK. How would everybody know? Being as ignorant as everybody is. People get it wrong – always – they tell me what they think I mean. Puffing themselves up – People! What do people know about art? Nothing. What do they know about themselves? Nothing. Critics! Do I work to amuse them? Can they judge me as equals? – when they are themselves without my gift. My chisels in their hands... My... Dead minds in unresponsive bodies. Imagine showing a Rembrandt to a blind man – pointing out subtleties of colour – the movement of light. Dear God! Why should I go on working? Why?

MAIA. You don't work any more. You don't call the rubbish you –

RUBEK. It's not rubbish –

MAIA. Endless portrait busts? Politicians – bankers – owners of factories? You immortalise the shame everybody would prefer to forget –

RUBEK. And I make a great deal of money at it. And it's not rubbish.

MAIA. Then what is it?

RUBEK. Something between art and... Anyway. Because I do it, it's not without merit.

Pause.

MAIA. It looks like rubbish to me.

RUBEK. Keeps my fingers supple. Like a pianist, a sculptor has to exercise. And I amuse myself – I cut secrets deep into the marble. Riddles the ignorant – the critics – can't decipher.

MAIA. What secrets?

RUBEK. My joke on them. 'Isn't it just like him?' they say – 'It's a remarkable likeness!' Dear God! Likeness! What is a likeness? If they had my eyes and mind they'd see beneath the glow of the marble not 'likeness' but the person himself – alive! Under the marble flesh of every politician, provincial mayor, or great achiever, I've revealed his bestial soul. This field marshal's a clumsy carthorse – that cabinet minister with the drooling jaws is a vicious dog lying stinking by the fire – an aristocrat with the pink eyelashes and white lardy flesh of a greasy pig – a stupid mule – a lumbering bull –

MAIA. All the fun of the farmyard.

RUBEK. Human animal nature. I shape them into the creatures they abuse. And how I make them pay. With my golden chisel. (*Drains his champagne*.)

MAIA (*fills glass*). What a wicked man you've become.

RUBEK. Makes me happy. Having money – masses of money – knowing I can always do exactly as I please for the rest of my life. (*Pause*.) Is that being happy?

MAIA. But don't forget what you promised.

RUBEK. What did I promise? You mean when I married you?

MAIA. You said I must go wherever you decided, but I could enjoy myself how I liked... And the other thing.

RUBEK. What other thing?

MAIA. The thing the Devil offered Christ.

RUBEK (*laughs*). Good Lord! Did I promise that? You too?

MAIA. Me too? Who else have you promised such –

RUBEK. I promised it to myself –

MAIA. Then it's to be yours and mine.

RUBEK. I'm sorry if I gave you that impression. I didn't mean it.

MAIA. What?

RUBEK. I never meant it. You are incapable of understanding it… I like the sound of the words – I like mountains. 'The Devil took him up into a high mountain and showed him all the glories of the world in a moment of time.' Actually, it's kingdoms not glories. I like the words. They have a magical ring to them. An incantation – it's what I used to say to my friends when we were little boys and I wanted them to come out and play: 'Come up into the high mountains and I'll show you all the kingdoms of the world!'

MAIA. It wasn't a game.

RUBEK (*making a joke of it*). No, and you're no little boy. It's amusing. Yes…

MAIA. I won't be laughed at.

RUBEK. No? (*Laughs.*)

MAIA. You've never shown me anything.

RUBEK. It would be a waste of my time.

MAIA. What else do you do but waste time –

RUBEK (*angry*). You have everything money can buy. It should be enough for a girl with nothing in her head.

MAIA. You said I would be your inspiration.

RUBEK. I deluded myself.

MAIA. You believed it once.

RUBEK. Then I married you. It was a long time ago.

MAIA (*bitter*). It's seemed a long time, has it? Four years.

RUBEK. It's beginning to feel like a very long time. (*Yawns.*)

MAIA. I detest you.

> MAIA *goes back to her chair; reads a paper; silence;* WAITERS *and* GUESTS *begin to appear.*

RUBEK. You have to weigh the loathing against the riches. (*Pause.*) Are you going to sulk?

MAIA. I'm ignoring you.

Enter the HOTEL MANAGER.

MANAGER. Good morning, madam. Professor.

MAIA. Good morning.

RUBEK *nods*.

MANAGER. I hope you're finding everything to your satisfaction.

MAIA. Yes. I was, anyway.

MANAGER. Excellent, excellent. One's first night in a strange bed... Professor?

RUBEK. Except that I can't sleep. Not at the moment.

MANAGER. Oh, I'm very sorry. A few weeks here at the health spa –

RUBEK. Who is it that – Was somebody out during the night? – Or is night exercise part of the treatment?

MANAGER (*surprised*). I can't think what you –

RUBEK. Well, there was –

MANAGER. Nobody would –

RUBEK. Somebody walking about outside my window?

MANAGER. I don't believe so.

MAIA. Ignore my husband. He dreams things.

RUBEK. I couldn't sleep so I got up and looked out of the window.

MANAGER. Well...

RUBEK. A white figure – down there in the trees.

MAIA. It wasn't a white figure. It was wearing a white dressing gown.

RUBEK. You saw it too, did you? How would you know what I saw?

MAIA. He thought it was a ghost.

RUBEK. You're ridiculous.

MANAGER. A lady or a gentleman?

RUBEK. A woman. Then another figure – darker – came up behind it.

MANAGER. Ah! Dressed in black?

RUBEK. Yes.

MANAGER. Behind the white figure? Close behind?

RUBEK. Yes.

MANAGER. Ah! I see.

RUBEK. What do you see?

MAIA. Don't tell me it *was* a ghost?

> *The* LADY IN WHITE (IRENA DE SATOFF) *and the* NUN *pass over the stage.*

RUBEK. Who is she?

MANAGER. A guest.

RUBEK. Foreign?

MANAGER. I think so.

RUBEK. What's her name?

MANAGER. The register says 'Madame de Satoff and companion.'

RUBEK. Satoff… Satoff…

MAIA. Do you know her, Rubek?

RUBEK. It sounds Russian – Eastern Europe anyway. What language do they speak?

MANAGER. To each other? – I couldn't say – a language I'm not familiar with. But her Norwegian is perfect so –

RUBEK. Her Norwegian? Never! Nobody speaks Norwegian except Norwegians –

MANAGER. I assure you, sir. Flawless. Perhaps with a trace of the north in it.

RUBEK. So you've had conversations?

MANAGER. Of course.

RUBEK *stares ahead and says nothing.*

MAIA. Was she one of your girls? Did she model for you?

RUBEK. My girls?

MAIA. From your past life. I imagine you had girls to model.

RUBEK. Ah. You imagine that, do you? I had only one. One was more than sufficient for every piece of work I've ever done. Then and since. Maybe even before, then and since.

MANAGER. Please excuse me. There's a gentleman over there I wish to avoid.

RUBEK. Who?

MANAGER. I believe it's Baron Ulfheim.

RUBEK. Ulfheim? 'The mighty hunter'?

MANAGER. Exactly.

RUBEK. So it is. I used to know him. And I can imagine why you'd want to avoid him.

MANAGER. Quite.

RUBEK. Is he coming here for a rest cure?

MANAGER. He comes every year – when he's setting off on his expeditions – I must go – (*Starts to.*)

ULFHEIM (*off*). Hey, you! Come back here... Didn't you hear me?

MANAGER. Sir?

Enter ULFHEIM, *and* LARS *his huntsman with hunting dogs.*

ULFHEIM. Where d'y'think you're going? Creeping away when I called –

MANAGER (*calmly*). Good morning, Baron. Did you come on the steamer?

ULFHEIM. Fool! Can't you see my yacht down there? (*To* LARS.) Here, boy.

LARS *comes closer, nervous;* ULFHEIM *grabs him by the hair and pulls his head about.*

Follow him – he'll show you where the kitchen is. He's a servant – don't let him put on airs and graces with you. You're my servant so you outrank him. He needs bones – hardly any meat – raw and bloody – keep 'em hungry, keep their senses sharp. Let's see your teeth.

LARS *shows his teeth.*

Get your own feed too while you're at it.

ULFHEIM *slaps* LARS*'s face half-affectionately but hard – he treats* LARS, *literally, like a dog.*

Go on – off. (*Hits him with his stick.*)

MANAGER. Will you come in to breakfast, Baron?

ULFHEIM. In there among the dead bluebottles? Sit with the corpses sucking at coffee cups?

MANAGER. As you wish, sir.

ULFHEIM. Get 'em to pack me a hamper. Just food – don't muck it about – and plenty of cognac. They know what I like.

MANAGER. Yes, Baron. I think we know what you like. Can I ask them to bring you anything, Professor? Madam? More coffee?

RUBEK. Not for me.

MAIA. No, thank you.

MANAGER *bows and goes.* LARS, *smiling, leads off the dogs.*

ULFHEIM (*half to himself*). This one ignores me now. Thrusting in with his betters –

RUBEK. Are you speaking to me? Or just about me?

ULFHEIM. Aren't you Rubek the sculptor?

RUBEK. Yes. And you are Ulfheim. I believe we've met.

ULFHEIM. Oho, we've met. Years ago. Before you became so high and mighty.

RUBEK (*smiling*). Come and join us.

MAIA. What do you hunt?

ULFHEIM. Bear if I can get 'em. In India tigers, pig – Africa lion, elephant. Here, wolves, women, elk – whatever's liveliest and most dangerous. Bears are best. (*Drinks from his flask.*)

MAIA. Why?

ULFHEIM. They come closest. (*Gets out his hunting knife, holds it up then puts it on the table.*) That close sometimes. (*Laughs.*) He does stone, I do bears. Both hard stuff to work with. Marble blocks, or muscle and sinew – both have to be hammered into shape – however much they struggle – however much they resist. We don't give up till we've beaten them. Do we, Rubek?

RUBEK (*deep in thought*). Hmmm.

ULFHEIM. Marble fights back, doesn't it?

RUBEK. Oh, yes. Art fights back.

ULFHEIM. Doesn't want to be hammered into life. It's just the opposite with a bear.

MAIA. Where are you going?

ULFHEIM. Ever been up into those mountains?

MAIA. No. My husband thinks mountains would be wasted on me.

ULFHEIM. I'll take you.

MAIA. We can't. We're off on a cruise. Round the islands and up to the Arctic.

ULFHEIM. Are you mad? Sitting in the damp mist, floating on rainwater? Steaming up a sewer? Would it give you pleasure?

MAIA. I don't believe it's pleasure my husband is looking for.

ULFHEIM. What is he looking for? An expedition into the mountains is what you need – just the place for boys and girls, eh, Professor? Clean crisp air. No dead people –

The NUN *crosses the stage and goes into the hotel.*

What did I tell you? Ravens are bad luck. Somebody's going to die.

RUBEK. Happens to us all. Sooner or later.

ULFHEIM. Philosopher, are you? No, people are dying. Dying is in the air. Where there's one of those circling, there's always some sickly half-rotten creature waiting to gasp out its last breath. I hate sickness. I wish sick people would hurry up and die.

MAIA. Have you never been ill yourself?

ULFHEIM. Never. But some of my loved ones have.

MAIA. Did you have to nurse them?

ULFHEIM. No. I shot them.

RUBEK. Shot them!

MAIA. Killed them?

ULFHEIM. I've never been known to miss.

MAIA. Killing people's against the law, isn't it?

ULFHEIM. They weren't people.

IRENA *comes and sits at a table.*

MAIA. But you said your loved ones.

ULFHEIM. I love my dogs.

MAIA. You love your dogs?

ULFHEIM. And they love me. When one of them's in pain – looks up at me from the bottom of his eyes – I kiss him goodbye and – bang! – seconds later he's young again – chasing the wind through the fields of yellow asphodel.

The NUN *comes out and leaves a tray with bread and a glass of milk in front of* IRENA.

Look at that. Milk and sops. A graveside offering. Do you want to see young Lars feed my dogs?

MAIA. Oh yes! May I? (*Smiles at* RUBEK.)

ULFHEIM. Crunching up the marrow bones – swallow them down – sick 'em up – gulp 'em down again. A dog's life. Come and watch if you like.

He goes; she follows.

Long pause.

RUBEK (*without moving or looking*). Irena?

Pause.

IRENA. I was.

RUBEK. Do you recognise me?

IRENA. You're still alive. Makes it easier for you.

RUBEK. I don't understand?

IRENA. Who's the girl?

RUBEK (*reluctantly*). Sitting here? Er... She's my wife. She –

IRENA. It's of no consequence.

RUBEK (*unsure*). No...

IRENA. Someone you acquired after I'd gone – once life was over.

RUBEK. Your life was over...? What do you mean?

IRENA. How's the child?

RUBEK. What? Irena –

IRENA. Our child – I believe it outlived me – became famous?

RUBEK. Oh 'our child'. Yes. (*Trying for a more normal form of conversation.*) Yes. It had quite a success – it's famous all over the world now. You must have read about it in the arts journals. Our child. That's what we used to call it –

IRENA. Earning for its father an international reputation.

RUBEK. Well, I owe it to you. Largely. Thank you... Irena.

Pause.

IRENA. Do you know what I should have done? (*Pause.*) Before I left you...

RUBEK. What?

IRENA. I wish I'd had the courage to destroy it.

RUBEK. Don't say that. You couldn't have done that.

IRENA. Not then. No. I could now. Now you disown my part in it.

RUBEK. You shouldn't have left me. Why *did* you leave me?

IRENA. You've no right to ask.

RUBEK. Was it for somebody else?

IRENA. Of course not. I had to get away – from somebody who took away my life then stopped needing me.

RUBEK (*standing*). I'm sorry. This is becoming unpleasant –

IRENA. Unpleasant?

RUBEK. Perhaps it's best if we...

IRENA. Why rake up the past? It's dead and gone. As I am.

RUBEK. I searched for you. For months.

IRENA. Good. I was hiding in the dark. While the bright lights were on our child.

RUBEK. They said you'd gone abroad?

IRENA. Yes. I've been all over the world. America.

RUBEK. What did you do?

IRENA. What did I do, what did I do? What didn't I do? Since you ask... Got a job in a music hall. Stripped naked, plucked and painted, on a revolving drum – 'The Living Statue, Gentlemen, so real you'd think she was flesh and blood – you'd almost believe she was alive!' I made good money. Selling my body. Whereas you never gave me a krone. Always broke, weren't you? Then I made a real fortune – with my body – ensnaring rich men. I could never trap you, though, could I, Arnold? You were pure. Pure and cold as art. (*Laughs.*)

RUBEK. But you married?

IRENA. A diplomat from Brazil. (*Smiles, staring into the past.*)
I drove him insane. That's not just a figure of speech. I
actually drove him to madness – quite deliberately. Well, to
be precise, when I saw it was beginning to happen, I helped
it along – I really began to work at it – made it into a game.
It was fun.

RUBEK. Where is he now?

IRENA. In the family vault.

RUBEK. He died?

IRENA. Men who fire bullets into their brains usually die.

RUBEK. He shot himself?

IRENA. He beat me to it.

RUBEK. Don't you feel any remorse?

IRENA. None.

RUBEK. Poor Satoff!

IRENA. Who?

RUBEK. Your husband – Satoff?

IRENA. It wasn't Satoff. Satoff's Russian – my second
husband.

RUBEK. Where is he?

IRENA. I don't know. Somewhere. Off with his gold mines. In
the caucuses, I think.

RUBEK. Is that where you live?

She looks at him and says nothing.

Is that where he lives?

IRENA. It's not really living. I'm killing him too. Very slowly –
cutting him to the brain –

RUBEK. Irena –

IRENA. On my bedside table I have a surgeon's knife. I
perform delicate operations –

RUBEK. Stop it, Irena!

IRENA. It's the truth –

RUBEK. It's not true! (*Pause; uncertain whether or not to stay.*) So… You never had children?

IRENA. Yes. I did.

RUBEK. Where are they?

IRENA. Can't you guess?

RUBEK. Irena!

IRENA. I got rid of them – as soon as they were born. One after another.

RUBEK. Don't think I don't know why you're saying these things –

IRENA. You should know. Only you know.

RUBEK (*rests his hands on the table and looks at her*). It's as if you're crumbling into pieces, Irena.

IRENA (*softly*). First we die. Then we fall into pieces. In fact, the process starts long before the breath leaves the body. How could you imagine my suffering? For years… I couldn't say truly if I were alive or dead. It didn't feel like being alive. They have a special garment – it's padded and they tie it very tight. Then, using a rubber tube and a funnel, they force opiates into you – give you terrifying dreams – and lower you into a tomb – cold – hardly any light – that's padded too – with bars and an iron door – so nobody hears you screeching and shrieking. No, they hear, but nobody comes… So… Was that being alive? Conscious, yes – Alive? I've not been brought back to life. At least I'm out of the tomb.

RUBEK. Do you blame me?

IRENA. Oh yes. I blame you.

RUBEK. Why?

IRENA. Because you are to blame. Maybe it was inevitable – maybe it was what you thought you needed to do. But I suffered. You were guilty. Sit down.

He does.

A little apart from each other. Just like old times.

RUBEK. It was the way it had to be. Then. I could not come closer.

IRENA. Oh?

RUBEK. You know why.

IRENA. Everything you took was for your art – gazing, studying – everything. All the secrets of my body. I was more naked than when I stood on my little drum. You took more than all those filthy men... You.

RUBEK. I never harmed you.

IRENA. Oh, you liar! Is that what you tell yourself? You destroyed my mind.

RUBEK. No!

IRENA. Yes! You did! You went into me – abused me –

RUBEK. Never! –

IRENA. Oh, but you were cunning! (*Softly.*) You pushed right inside but you never touched my body.

RUBEK. If I'd allowed myself –

IRENA. I would have killed you too. Perhaps. I wonder...

RUBEK. I could not risk breaking the spell. My art –

IRENA (*laughs contemptuously*). Your art! It *is* what you tell yourself –

RUBEK. Everything else had to be sacrificed. For *Judgement Day*... (*Lost in remembrance*.) Out of the sleep of death a young woman awakening –

IRENA. Our child –

RUBEK. Immaculate – noble – untouched by the world... And I found you... You were so – exactly – right. And you wanted it too. No! You knew exactly what you were doing. You left your home, your family to come to me – willingly – joyfully –

IRENA. I was like a child – reborn in innocence –

RUBEK. That's what I needed from you – innocence – that's what was so useful to me. Something pure and hard… Unreachable. To possess that, I had to fix it – clay first, then in marble. Nature is fleeting – nothing… like sunlight passing over a meadow on a cloudy day. To have truth – eternity – beauty must become art. I was very young, Irena – a child myself. I knew nothing of the world. Women – the power they had frightened me. Oh, I could so easily have given in. You were so beautiful! But I made myself believe that if I let my body master me – or even dwelt upon the imagination of it – I'd lose the magic. The work would be a failure… I still think it may have been true.

IRENA (*a degree of scorn*). Art first. Let flesh and blood manage as best it can.

RUBEK. Art was supreme. Everything else – everything in nature took second place. Blame me if you like.

IRENA. So the magic worked.

RUBEK. It did. Together we made it work. Thank you. I fixed you in marble… as you were then.

IRENA (*places her hands on the table and leans back*). And then I was over and done with.

RUBEK. Irena!

IRENA. Of no further use.

RUBEK. Nonsense!

IRENA. Liar. (*Laughs.*) You'd used me up. The flower faded. You had to find a newer vision.

RUBEK. I never did.

IRENA. Other girls to model –

RUBEK. You were much more than that.

IRENA (*a look of scorn and disbelief then silence as she considers it*). What are you working on at the moment?

Unseen the NUN *takes up a position where she can watch* IRENA.

RUBEK. Nothing. Rubbish.

IRENA. With that vulgar girl? Is she your Muse of Mediocrity?

RUBEK (*angry*). She's a knife in my heart. (*Pause.*) Tomorrow we leave on an Arctic cruise. Thinking about the cold depresses me.

IRENA. Don't go then. You should climb up into the mountains. As high as you please. Up into the light.

RUBEK. Is that where you're going?

IRENA. Would you come with me?

RUBEK. I wonder if I dare.

IRENA. There's nothing stopping you.

Enter MAIA.

MAIA. I know what you'll say, Rubek – Oh, you have a new friend.

RUBEK (*stands*). No, an old friend.

MAIA. I've decided I'm not going on that dreary steamer. You can if you like –

RUBEK. Why not?

MAIA. Because I want to go up into the mountains – and the forest. I just have to. (*Pleading.*) Please, please, please say 'yes', Rubek. I'll do anything – anything you want – but let me go.

RUBEK. This can't be your idea.

MAIA. No, it's Ulfheim. He's a dreadful man! But he makes it sound so savage and mysterious – the wildness of the forest – the terror in the mountains – it's probably all lies, but he's cast a spell on me and now I want to see for myself – even if it's just to prove he's lying. Do let me go, Rubek. Oh, please!

RUBEK. Well, why not? I may come too.

MAIA (*too quickly*). You don't have to. Not if you don't want to.

RUBEK. I do want to.

MAIA. Well... Thank you. I'll go and tell him, shall I?

RUBEK. If you like.

MAIA. Oh, thank you, thank you, thank you, Rubek! (*Tries to take his hand but he won't let her.*) You're so sweet and indulgent this morning. (*Runs off.*)

RUBEK. We might meet then... up there in the mountains.

IRENA. Good. It's taken me so long to find you.

RUBEK. You've actually been looking for me? How long?

IRENA (*a bitter smile*). You stole something of mine – stole it and kept it. When I found it gone, I began my search.

RUBEK (*bows*). Three – four years of your youth.

IRENA. More precious than that.

RUBEK. What was it? (*Pause.*) Whatever it was, I gave you so much in return – I worshipped you.

IRENA. You worshipped yourself and your art.

RUBEK. I loved you.

IRENA. It wasn't enough. For what you stole from me...

RUBEK. What did I steal?

IRENA. And since you took it I've been desolate – an empty shell. (*Looks hard at him.*) You were the death of me, Arnold.

The NUN *waits for* IRENA *then follows her in.*

RUBEK (*whispers*). Irena.

ACT TWO

Higher up the mountain. A hill with a stone seat. A mountain
stream divides the scene. The sounds of children playing
happily. Just before sunset. RUBEK, *a shawl over his*
shoulders, sits on the seat, watching the children. MAIA *enters*
wearing walking clothes, and carrying a staff. She jumps over
the stream and climbs up the hill to the bench.

MAIA. I looked all over for you.

RUBEK. Back at the hotel?

MAIA. L'Hotel des Mouches Mortes.

RUBEK. You missed lunch.

MAIA. We had a picnic.

RUBEK. We?

MAIA. With Ulfheim. And Lars.

RUBEK. Dangerous company. I hope you took the dogs as
    chaperones?

MAIA. We're going out again in the morning.

RUBEK. After bears?

MAIA. Anything we can find worth a bullet.

RUBEK. Is a bear worth a bullet?

MAIA. What, up here? Don't parade your ignorance.

RUBEK. No bears then. What about wolves?

MAIA. The bears are down there in the thick forests. Away
    from humans.

RUBEK. And you've planned an expedition for the morning?

MAIA. Actually, we may set off this evening. If that's all right.

RUBEK. Do as you like.

MAIA. Lars will be with us, of course. And the dogs.

RUBEK. How tedious for you. (*Changing subject.*) Do you have to sprawl? There's a perfectly good bench here.

MAIA. I'm happy where I am.

RUBEK. You've worn yourself out.

MAIA. I believe I have.

RUBEK. You're unused to physical exercise. After violent activity comes complete collapse.

MAIA. Why are you watching those damn children? I wish they'd shut up.

RUBEK. Their moments of harmony sometimes assume a mystical significance. It makes all the yelling and screaming tolerable.

MAIA. Can't you ever stop!

RUBEK. What?

MAIA. Boring me! With art.

RUBEK. I'm an artist – what do you expect? I hope I always will be.

MAIA (*turning away from him*). He hasn't an inch of art in his whole hard body.

RUBEK. Who hasn't?

MAIA. Ulfheim.

RUBEK (*laughs*). I think we can safely agree about that.

MAIA. He's very beautiful though. In such an ugly sort of way. (*Pulls up some heather and throws it away.*) It's a terrible ugliness – hypnotic… Ughhh!

RUBEK. No wonder you're off to the woods with him.

MAIA. No wonder… I find you ugly too.

RUBEK. Do you?

MAIA. I've always thought so.

RUBEK. *Tempus edax rerum* – especially beauty. I'm an old man.

MAIA. I'm not talking about your looks. It's in your eyes – the miserly ugliness of a man who's given up. You no longer care for anything. Certainly not for me.

RUBEK. Don't I?

MAIA. You don't watch me any more. Hardly. And if you do there's a nasty glint in your eye. As if you want to poison me.

RUBEK. I'd never resort to poison. Come and sit here. (*Slaps his knee.*)

MAIA (*starts to get up*). What, on your knee? It's been ages since you behaved like –

RUBEK. No – they'd see us from the hotel. Here. Come here. (*Indicates the bench.*)

MAIA. No. (*Flops down again.*)

RUBEK. Do you know why I suggested this trip?

MAIA. You said it would do me good. Obviously you had other reasons.

RUBEK. Which were?

MAIA. How should I know? Probably because you'd arranged to accidentally bump into the walking corpse.

RUBEK. Who?

MAIA. That woman.

RUBEK. Madame de Satoff?

MAIA. She's always lurking. It can't be an accident that she's followed us up here.

RUBEK. Can't it?

MAIA. I'm sure there was something between you. In Ancient Times. Before you met me.

RUBEK. She was long forgotten before I met you.

MAIA. Can you just write people off like that, Rubek? Draw a line under them and forget them?

RUBEK. Yes. (*Sharply.*) You wouldn't believe how easily I can do it. (*Hard.*) Once I've made up my mind to have done with them.

MAIA. A woman who inspired you?

RUBEK. Surely. If I no longer need her.

MAIA. A woman who was naked for you?

RUBEK. I'm an artist. Flesh and blood means very little. (*Change of tone.*) And how could I possibly have guessed she would turn up at the spa?

MAIA. I don't know. Perhaps you didn't but then you saw her name in the register.

RUBEK. I didn't know her name – her married name – until the manager mentioned it. You know that – you were there.

MAIA. Oh, I don't know anything. I'm sick of guessing games. So why did you bring us here?

RUBEK. Why indeed! I suppose we'll have to face it sooner or later.

MAIA (*stifling a fit of laughter*). You do look ridiculous when you're trying to be serious.

RUBEK. Perhaps I have been taking myself too seriously. Perhaps there's no need.

MAIA. Now I'm intrigued.

RUBEK. Not worried?

MAIA. Not a bit.

RUBEK. At the spa you said you thought I couldn't be still, and I hated everybody?

MAIA. It was true.

RUBEK. Why is that, do you think?

MAIA. You're sick of my… conversation?

RUBEK. The interminable drivel you talk – yes, that's part of it.

MAIA. Well, we've hardly been apart for, what – four – nearly five years? I…

RUBEK. Go on.

MAIA (*suddenly depressed*). Well, you are very boring you know, Rubek. You despise the few friends I have left – you won't share any of your interests with me – I know nothing about art anyway – and I can't say I've ever wanted to. (*Impatient.*) God knows you make it sound so unnatural and dull!

RUBEK. In five years you've never said anything worth remembering.

MAIA. I don't have anything very profound to contribute. But the alternative is silence.

RUBEK. What's wrong with silence? You're a waste of my time.

MAIA. You don't have much time left, do you, Rubek? Is that why you're beginning to panic?

RUBEK. Yes. I don't think I can bear much more.

MAIA. Well, if you want rid of me, just say the word.

RUBEK. 'Rid of you'? I don't want rid of you.

MAIA. It sounds as if you do... Shall I pack my bags?

RUBEK. Is that meant to be a threat?

MAIA. How could it be? To threaten you with something you want.

RUBEK. No, you're right. But I don't want to be rid of you – I'm not that cruel. Though... things will have to change.

MAIA. How?

RUBEK. Well, there's no need for us to separate.

MAIA (*scorn*). You just want to play the field a bit before you drop dead? Is that it?

RUBEK (*smiles*). Well...

MAIA. Oh, say it!

RUBEK. I need somebody I feel at peace with.

MAIA. And I won't do?

RUBEK. No, you most certainly will not do. Not in the way I mean. I need somebody who can be the other half of me... who is in harmony with – I can't say it in any other way – who understands my art.

MAIA (*sadly*). That's never going to be me. (*Smiles*.)

RUBEK. No, my dear. I'm afraid it's not.

MAIA (*angry*). Good! I'm glad it's not me!

RUBEK. I knew when I married you that you were deficient in... (*Stops himself*.)

MAIA. So, who is it to be?

RUBEK. What do you mean?

MAIA. I'm not a fool – I'm way ahead of you.

RUBEK. Then tell me.

MAIA. Love from the Grave. The ancient model of your adolescent dreams. The one – (*Breaking off*.) By the way – you know that all the people in the hotel are convinced she's insane?

RUBEK. Oh? What do people in the hotel say about you and your...

MAIA. My what? My what? (*Pause*.) Anyway, am I right? Is it her we're discussing?

RUBEK. I thought I had no need of her – and yes, I wrote her off – or at least I was planning to. But then she left me. And... I looked all over for her. For months, and years...

MAIA. And when you couldn't find her you thought you'd make do with me?

RUBEK. Yes. I did. I finished my masterpiece – *Judgement Day* – it was exhibited all over the world and it made me famous – and very, very rich. But I soon got bored with it all – the laurels – the applause. My genius had deserted me – all I had left was skill – technique... I was desolate. I hid in the deep dark forests...

MAIA. Like a stinking old bear. And started carving marble heads of lord mayors and Freemasons.

RUBEK. My farmyard faces – yes, but...

MAIA. But what?

RUBEK. I'd lost my faith. I began to think that art was a fraud. That there was no such thing as genius. Only technique – craft – clever drudgery. The rest was meaningless – trickery – fraud, in fact... I no longer wanted anything to do with it.

MAIA. So what did you want instead?

RUBEK. To enjoy myself. To the full.

MAIA. I shouldn't think you'd know where to start.

RUBEK. Perhaps you're right. I just know I wanted to live in the sun – with beauty – what the lower orders call the good things of life – I didn't want to spend the rest of my days in penury – in a dank studio up to my eyes in clay, and marble chippings.

MAIA. You sold out. Good for you.

RUBEK. I grew rich and lazy and bought the villa on the lake and the big house and all the rest of it –

MAIA. Including me. I'm part of 'all the rest of it', aren't I? – and you swore to hold me and have me and endow me with all your worldly goods –

RUBEK (*laughing*). – and take you into a high mountain and show you all the kingdoms of the world!

MAIA. And you never have.

RUBEK (*angry*). You want too much. You're pure greed, aren't you? Do you know what terrifies me most?

MAIA. Being stuck with me for ever.

RUBEK. Right.

MAIA. Heartless.

RUBEK. You haven't the least idea –

MAIA. I haven't a single idea in my stupid head! Next?

RUBEK. My mind works at such a pace – it consumes everything in its path – everything ordinary – in the few years since our marriage I've lived a whole tedious life with you – I've used you up – I've used everything up – everything that money can buy – villas – houses – every country we've visited – idleness – every luxury – every pleasure – every vice – it's just not enough for me! I want more! There must be more to it. I have to create again – find a way back to my art! To the peace of mind that comes in knowing the world is right. That's why you won't do, Maia. I can't do with you any longer... not just you.

MAIA (*calmly, ironically*). So that's all it is... You're tired of me?

RUBEK. I'm sick to death of you! And this wretched, meaningless, slow, slow nightmare life – I'm so pointless I've stopped *being*! Dear God! (*Controls himself.*) I'm sorry. You're right. I'm heartless and cruel. It's not your fault. It's just that I think I've found what I want and it's not you.

MAIA. We'll separate.

RUBEK. Would you care?

MAIA. Do I have a choice?

RUBEK. Yes. We could...

MAIA. What about the Living Dead?

RUBEK. I suppose I must have known – the shape of her – that night I looked out of the window back at the spa.

MAIA. Oh.

RUBEK. What made me look out? In here and here – (*His heart and his brain.*) is a little treasure chest. Locked in it is my genius – my artist's vision. That woman, Maia, ran off with the only key. I'm helpless. Time's running out and I can't get at the treasure.

MAIA (*subtle smile*). She'd better get to work then – picking your lock?

RUBEK. What? I –

MAIA. It's why she's here, isn't it? She's after your treasure.

RUBEK. I've said nothing to her.

MAIA. Who cares!

RUBEK. Easy enough to say –

MAIA. Talk to her. If you want her. You needn't worry about me.

RUBEK. What do you mean?

MAIA. I can look after myself. I'll go and live at the villa if things become difficult. Though I don't see why they should. The other house is so big – three people ought to be able to keep out of each other's way.

RUBEK (*not convinced*). Do you think it would work?

MAIA. How should I know?

RUBEK. What if it doesn't?

MAIA. Then we'll have to think of something else. More permanent. No – don't worry about me. I like the idea of being free. Free. Free... Oh God! Here comes a funeral procession.

RUBEK. Where?

MAIA. Coming up the path. She looks like a carving on a tombstone.

RUBEK (*to himself*). She's the resurrection and the life.

MAIA. What's that supposed to mean?

RUBEK. An explanation would be wasted on you.

MAIA. Explain it to her then.

RUBEK. Where are you going?

MAIA. That's my affair, isn't it? Now.

Goes; she meets IRENA.

Professor Rubek's waiting over there – he'd like a word with you.

IRENA *says nothing*.

I think he wants you to unlock his baubles.

IRENA. What?

MAIA. Oh, he'll explain.

IRENA. If I can help him –

MAIA. He seems to think you're the only one who can.

She jumps over the stream and exits. IRENA *does not cross the stream but sits. After a while,* RUBEK *comes down.*

IRENA. You've been waiting for me.

RUBEK. For some time.

IRENA. And all that time I've been asleep. Dreaming. Down there.

RUBEK. Well, you're awake now.

IRENA *shakes her head.*

A new day. The sun… rising.

IRENA (*looks at the setting sun*). It isn't. It won't.

RUBEK. Now that I've found you –

IRENA. Found my grave – I am out of my grave –

RUBEK. A resurrection.

IRENA. No. Just out of my grave.

He crosses the stream to her; tries to adopt a more realistic mode of conversation.

RUBEK. What have you been doing today, Irena?

IRENA. I've been for a walk – (*Pointing.*) over there on the mountainside. Bleak – no life –

RUBEK. You're alone this afternoon. Where's your… companion?

IRENA. Watching me. (*Smiles.*)

RUBEK. Where? How can she be?

IRENA. I'm never out of her sight. (*Looks around; whispers.*) She'll have to die. One fine morning – I'll find a way.

RUBEK. You wouldn't –

IRENA. I would! (*Smiles.*) Half a chance – that's all I ask.

RUBEK. But why?

IRENA. She dabbles in the black art. She can transform herself into my shadow.

RUBEK (*trying to humour her*). No. We all have a shadow –

IRENA. Except me. (*With force.*) I'm my own shadow. Do you understand what I'm saying to you? Or do you prefer to think I'm mad? Is that easier for you?

RUBEK (*sadly*). You're not mad.

IRENA. Is it so difficult to look at me, Arnold?

RUBEK (*softly*). I don't know. But I'm afraid to.

IRENA. Why are you afraid?

RUBEK. With you it's a shadow. With me it's my conscience.

IRENA. Oh! (*Laughs with joy – as if released from some great burden.*)

RUBEK. What's the matter? What have I said? Irena!

IRENA. I'm all right – it's all right now. (*Makes an effort to stabilise herself; breathes deeply.*) Yes! I've escaped them for the moment. Let's sit – yes – sit down. Talk to me.

RUBEK. I wish I could.

IRENA. Try. I've come so far to be with you. From a faraway land – beyond your imagination –

RUBEK (*smiles sadly*). From a faraway land…

IRENA. Home – to my loved ones.

RUBEK. Home. Where is home?

IRENA. Did you think of me every day? Did you always hope you'd see me again?

RUBEK. How could I hope? What right had I to hope?

IRENA. No, you couldn't. You didn't know…

RUBEK. And there was no one else?

IRENA. Who?

RUBEK. You didn't leave me for someone else?

IRENA. It was for your own sake. Is that too difficult for you to understand?

RUBEK. It is.

IRENA (*suddenly rapid, very lucid*). Everything was for you.
Every impulse was towards you. You had my soul – you
could have had my body. And when the child was finished –
in the clay at least – don't forget, I've never seen it in the
marble – and remember it was you that used to call it 'our
child' – '*our* child' – you took even more from me. You took
away my rights in it. I was required to give up the part I had
in it. You demanded that sacrifice – all your own work! – It
was as if I'd never existed.

RUBEK (*bowing his head*). Since then I've been worthless.

IRENA. Yes, without me! (*Angry.*) That's exactly what I had to
make you understand. You can do nothing without me. I
wanted the realisation to dawn upon you – very slowly and
painfully – that you'd never create anything of worth ever
again.

RUBEK. You were jealous of my art.

IRENA. Your art! Our child! It wasn't jealousy, it was hatred.

RUBEK. Hatred?

IRENA. You sucked the warmth – the life out of me – oh so
casually – because you needed my soul to make into art.

RUBEK. No! You gave yourself – you were as dedicated as I
was. We made a holiness of it –

IRENA. Sanctimonious fool!

RUBEK. Why am I – ?

IRENA. I never gave a damn for your art. I was unmoved by it
when you first spoke to me and unmoved even when I saw
what you could do.

RUBEK. But what of the artist?

IRENA. I despise artists. They choke the life out of us.

RUBEK. But –

IRENA. Yes. And you most of all – the artist in you. I was
naked for you – waiting for you – hating you –

RUBEK. I don't believe you –

IRENA. It's true! I hated you! Everything I was – naked in front of you – and you could stand there completely unmoved –

RUBEK (*laughs*). Unmoved! If you believed that –

IRENA. In control then – so coldly and insufferably self-controlled! Debasing a woman – *me* into art. Always a mere artist – an unsexed artist – Never any youth and blood in you – never moving in me like a lover – never growing into a man! (*Anger is replaced by tenderness.*) I did love our child though... Then. Watching it take shape and life from the clay. It was our creation. As much mine as yours.

RUBEK (*sadly*). It was a kind of truth. Our truth.

IRENA (*cold*). It's what we created together I've come to find. Not you.

RUBEK (*worried*). The sculpture?

IRENA. 'Our child.'

RUBEK. But, Irena... You want to see the finished object? In the marble?

IRENA. Cold marble –

RUBEK. Well, you can't. Not easily. It's in America. In a museum.

IRENA *absorbs this information.*

You always hated museums – I remember you saying – 'Graveyards', you used to call them.

IRENA. I shall have to make a pilgrimage. That work contains my soul – and my child's.

RUBEK (*worried*). You must never see it again, Irena. I beg you – put it out of your mind.

IRENA. Ah! No – Put *me* out of my mind – You're afraid the sight of it will put me out of my mind again.

RUBEK. It's possible – I mean, it wasn't even finished when you left –

IRENA. It *was* finished!

RUBEK. But –

IRENA. It was finished. That's why I could leave you. Because we'd finished it. In the clay.

RUBEK. But... I went on with it.

IRENA (*unseen, pulls out a knife*). Without me? You hurt our child?

RUBEK. Hurt? I never saw –

IRENA. Good – No mother likes to think –

RUBEK. But I don't know what you'd make of it now. In its final state. In the marble...

IRENA. Describe it to me.

RUBEK. *Judgement Day*... It had been taking shape in my mind long before I met you. But when we did meet I understood at once how I could use you – work with you – You brought everything together. I was very young. Innocent. My imagination was uncorrupted by any worldliness. The vision of *Judgement* I had was of beauty – as a young girl – untouched – standing pure in the light of Heaven – without sin – no taint of evil to burn away –

IRENA (*excited*). Oh yes! That was our work. That's how I stand in marble now.

RUBEK. Yes. (*Hesitates*.) Well... More or less...

IRENA (*contempt*). More or less? You made changes? After the clay?

RUBEK. After you left me... In the years that... I began to understand the world, Irena. *Judgement Day* took on a newer meaning – a larger scale – it lost its simplicity.

IRENA. Go on.

RUBEK. I wanted to show the world to itself – show life. It became a much larger project –

IRENA (*contempt*). A project! (*Draws the knife behind her back*.)

RUBEK. It had to grow, Irena – It took me over – I wasn't in control. The base where you stood was enlarged – I wanted to show the earth bulging and splitting as the dead crept out of their graves – human bodies with animal masks – it was how I saw them –

IRENA (*fighting to keep control*). But I still... I am innocence... Innocence is central to it – exulting in the light –

RUBEK. Yes. (*Means 'no' or 'not quite'.*) But in terms of composition... The piece required... Not exactly in the centre.

IRENA. So I'm just another figure? Exulting in the light.

RUBEK. Actually, there's more misery in the face now. My newer vision required that.

IRENA (*stands*). And that's how you see life now, is it?

RUBEK. Yes.

IRENA. Just another figure – misery in the face – that's what you fixed in the marble. (*Unsheathes the knife.*)

RUBEK. It's how I saw it.

IRENA. A judgement. You've just passed sentence on yourself.

RUBEK. Judgement?

RUBEK *looks up; she hides the knife.*

IRENA. You've corrupted the vision. We were all in that single figure – my soul – you – the child. We were truth – unassailable – for ever.

RUBEK (*looks at her for a moment then looks away*). I put myself in the work too. Kneeling at my graveside – by a stream – it could be here – still half in the earth – weighed down with guilt and shame. Portrait of a wasted life. I try to wash the clay from my hands – but I can't. Can't get out of hell. There's no resurrection.

IRENA. Failure! Poet!

RUBEK. Poet?

IRENA. You're feeble and sentimental – too ready to forgive yourself your lifetime of self-love. Spoilt child! Crybaby! You shipwreck my life and soul, and in penance you make a little stone model of yourself shedding a few tears and you light a candle in front of it! (*Smiles.*) And now you think you're free of me? You've paid your debts.

RUBEK. What else could I do? I'm weak. I can't help my art.

IRENA (*angry*). Poet! (*Suddenly laughs and relaxes and strokes his hair.*) Spoilt child. Crybaby. Poet.

RUBEK (*like a spoilt child*). Stop calling me that!

IRENA. Poet! There's something slimy and fey and irresponsible in the word. All the limpness and vice in a man can be excused if he's a poet – is that what you think? Because you're a poet you think you can put yourself above life? Certainly above me. (*Sadly.*) I was as guilty as you for letting you get away with it. For letting you lead. For denying my spirit in order to make myself your accomplice – lending you my strength. I shall never forgive myself.

RUBEK. That's not how it was at all, Irena. You must remember. There was such beauty – a clarity of vision – innocence. I've never been happy since.

IRENA. Do you remember what you said to me – the day it was finished in the clay?

RUBEK. No. What did I say?

IRENA. You're sure you don't remember?

RUBEK. Not exactly – no.

IRENA. You took my hands – drew me close to you – I was tingling with excitement – and you said: 'Thank you, Irena – thank you, thank you. This has been a most enjoyable and profitable association for me.'

RUBEK. 'Association'? Did I say 'association'? It's not a word I'd normally use.

IRENA. 'Association.'

RUBEK (*trying to make a joke of it*). Well, it was! In a way.

IRENA. So I left. Packed my bags and left. 'Association' was quite a heavy word to carry.

RUBEK. I didn't intend it like that. You misinterpreted me. Everything has to be so serious with you.

IRENA. Yes, it does. Oh, let's forget serious things! (*Throws the red petals of a rock rose into the stream.*) Swim away, little birds.

RUBEK. What sort of birds are they?

IRENA. Flamingos.

RUBEK. Flamingos can't swim.

IRENA. Seagulls.

RUBEK. With red legs and beaks? Yes, I suppose they could be. (*Throws in a leaf or two.*) I launch my little boats to follow them.

IRENA. I hope you're not out to shoot my birds.

RUBEK. I can't stand hunters. (*Smiling.*) Our game.

IRENA (*throwing petals*). Our game.

RUBEK. We could be back at our cottage on the lake.

IRENA. All those years ago. Yes. (*A shaft of hatred in her voice.*) It was an interesting association.

RUBEK (*ignoring the barb*). I seem to remember it was water lilies then.

IRENA. Yes. My lilies were swans in those days.

RUBEK. And dock-leaf boats.

IRENA. You were Lohengrin. I was your swan.

RUBEK. What?

IRENA. You used to say… I was the swan who drew your boat.

RUBEK. Did I? Perhaps. Look at your seagulls.

IRENA (*laughs*). And your ships have all run aground.

RUBEK. Let's launch some more. (*Throws leaves; pause.*) I bought that little cottage on Lake Taunitz, you know…

IRENA. Did you?

RUBEK. One day I happened to notice I was a very rich man. So I bought it.

IRENA. Is that where you live? In our cottage?

RUBEK. No. I had the cottage pulled down. I built a huge villa on the land. Splendid formal gardens. We… I usually spend the summer there.

IRENA. With that woman?

RUBEK (*almost defiantly*). My wife – yes.

IRENA. I was always happy on the lake.

RUBEK. But...

IRENA. Where have our lives gone? Wasted away.

RUBEK. If only we could have them back.

IRENA (*laughs at his naivety; says nothing for a while*). Look at the sun. Red-gold in the heather – like fire.

RUBEK. Ah! When did I last watch the sun set?

IRENA. Or rise.

RUBEK. I don't think I've ever seen a sunrise on the mountains.

IRENA (*smiling; lost in memories*). I did once. It was the most beautiful thing ever.

RUBEK. Where?

IRENA. Up there – where you promised I should see all the kingdoms of the world. If...

RUBEK. If?

IRENA. If I believed in you. If I would fall down and worship you. (*Silent for a moment; then softly.*) Artfully tempted by the Devil... And I did fall down... I watched the sun rise.

RUBEK. You could live by the lake again.

IRENA (*scorn*). With the other woman? A harem?

RUBEK. With me. As we used to be – working together. Unlock the good in me, Irena.

IRENA. I haven't the key. I don't believe there is a key.

RUBEK. Help me – I want to be alive.

IRENA. Be childlike again? It's not possible. I'm not your resurrection. Just dreams...

RUBEK, *angry; then resigned; throws leaves*. IRENA *throws petals*.

RUBEK. Well then... All we can do is put away serious things – just keep on playing.

IRENA. Playing… playing… waiting…

They throw leaves and petals; enter MAIA, *followed by* ULFHEIM *and* LARS. RUBEK *watches them.*

It's your other woman.

RUBEK. She's probably his by now.

MAIA (*calling*). Sweet dreams, Rubek. I'm off on an expedition.

RUBEK. Where to?

MAIA. A hunting expedition. I'm going to catch myself a life worth living.

RUBEK (*mocking*). Bring one back for me!

MAIA. I'll bring you something.

RUBEK. Good hunting then! Good luck!

ULFHEIM. Hey! Don't you know it's bad luck to wish a hunter luck?

RUBEK. Bad luck then! To both of you.

ULFHEIM. Thanks! We'll shoot you a bear or two.

MAIA. Or a buzzard – I'll wing an old buzzard for you and you can model it into a self-portrait.

RUBEK (*with a bitter laugh*). Very much your style, Maia. Blasting away at the mysteries of life. Womanhood red in tooth and claw.

MAIA. Well, I have to do something to kill time. Waste it or make it fly. (*Laughs at him.*) Enjoy yourselves – enjoy your wild summer night under the stars. Or will it be more like a Night on the Bare Mountain? (*Laughs.*)

Unseen the NUN *appears, watching them.*

RUBEK. Thank you! (*Jovially.*) I wish you both all the bad luck in the world – fall down crevasses and be eaten by the bears you hunt!

ULFHEIM (*laughing*). That's the idea! Now you're getting it! Thanks, Rubek!

MAIA (*laughing*). Yes, thank you, Rubek! Thank you! Bye!

They go.

RUBEK. A wild summer night under the stars. If we were still young and alive…

IRENA (*sneers*). Is that what you want? Wild summer nights?

RUBEK. Irena –

IRENA. With me?

RUBEK. Oh yes.

IRENA (*ironic smile*). Shall I fall down and worship you?

RUBEK. Oh, Irena…

IRENA (*feeling for the knife; smiling bitterly; cracked voice*). You wish to renew our association? (*Suddenly; whispering.*) Keep your voice down. Don't look.

RUBEK (*whispers*). What's the matter?

IRENA. She's spying on us.

RUBEK. Where? (*Turns involuntarily.*) Dear God!

IRENA. I must go. No – stay there. Come tonight. We'll go up there onto the mountainside and watch the dawn break.

RUBEK. Will you wait for me – here?

IRENA. Yes.

RUBEK. One summer night on the wild mountain… We could have had it all, Irena. I threw it away and you let me – watched me do it.

IRENA. One day we'll know just how much we've thrown away… But only – only when…

RUBEK. When will we know it?

IRENA. On the day of our resurrection, I suppose.

RUBEK. And what is there to know?

IRENA. That life's an illusion – just a trick of the light. There's no life. We don't exist.

She goes down the hill, followed by the NUN. RUBEK *sits by the stream, not moving.*

ACT THREE

*A narrow path at the edge of a precipice on a sheer
mountainside. Snow-capped peaks are seen through the mist. A
distant, half-ruined mountain hut. Dawn is breaking but the sun
has not yet risen. Thin icy light. Distant thunder.* MAIA *enters,
followed by* ULFHEIM, *half-furious, half-laughing.*

MAIA. No – let me go! Get your hands off me!

ULFHEIM. Vicious! Show your teeth. Do you like to bite –

MAIA. Let go.

ULFHEIM. I don't want to let go.

MAIA. I'm staying here then – not moving. Go on without me.

ULFHEIM. Why? When I've got you where I want you?

MAIA. I'll throw myself over the edge if you try anything.

ULFHEIM. Right! Come on then – let's see if you dare. It's a
  sheer drop down there – a mountain goat would think twice
  about using that path.

MAIA. So this is your idea of hunting!

ULFHEIM. The best! Yes – it's my idea of sport.

MAIA. Sport!

ULFHEIM. The chase, the struggle, the *coup de grâce*.

MAIA. Is that why you slipped the dogs back there?

ULFHEIM. Is it?

MAIA. So Lars would have to go after them? To get him out of
  the way?

ULFHEIM. Why should I want Lars out of the way? He's quite
  a sport himself.

MAIA. I don't want to hear –

ULFHEIM. It will take ages to catch up with them. Lars knows what's expected of him – when he's wanted and when to keep away.

MAIA. I'm sure he does.

ULFHEIM. He's a good boy. Knows what I like.

MAIA. I know what you're like.

ULFHEIM. Oh?

MAIA. Like an old satyr – half man, half goat.

ULFHEIM. Which half's goat?

MAIA. The legs. And – there –

ULFHEIM. What about the horns?

MAIA. Yes – those ugly little horns –

ULFHEIM. Little? Have a closer look.

MAIA. I don't need to. I can see quite plainly.

ULFHEIM (*takes out a dog's lead*). You'd better hurry then.

MAIA. What are you doing!

ULFHEIM. I'll have to put you on a leash.

MAIA. Are you mad!

ULFHEIM. If you won't walk to heel…

> *They are half-laughing, half-serious; she lets him start; then she shoves him away.*

MAIA. Get off me! You're supposed to be a baron and you can't even behave like a gentleman. (*Shoves him again and sits up.*) Where's this hunting lodge you told me about?

ULFHEIM (*angry; pointing*). There.

MAIA. That pigsty?

ULFHEIM (*laughing*). Well, more than one princess has found the accommodation to her liking.

MAIA. Yes – your disgusting story. The princess who woke up and found she was being deflowered by a bear.

ULFHEIM. Deflowered! Deflowered! I don't think that was the word I used. But, yes, it was in that very hut. (*Distant thunder.*) Shall we go up?

MAIA. D'you think I'm out of my mind? I wouldn't set foot in there. Ugh!

ULFHEIM. Nonsense! It's the perfect place to spend a summer's night – or the whole summer, if that's what you want.

MAIA. I want to get back down to the hotel before people start waking up.

ULFHEIM. I don't think it could be managed.

MAIA. Oh, you'll manage. I'm sure you know a way down.

ULFHEIM. There's a track, as I said. But it's dangerous. More of a climb – and it's a sheer drop as you can see. One false step –

MAIA. I'll risk it.

ULFHEIM. Well, if you think you dare.

MAIA (*afraid*). I'm not afraid. Come on! Or I'll go without you.

ULFHEIM (*not moving*). You'd never make it without my help.

MAIA (*frightened*). Then help me!

ULFHEIM. I could take you on my back.

MAIA. Don't be ridiculous –

ULFHEIM. Or you could lie on your back and I'll take you –

MAIA. Don't start that again! (*Shoves him away.*)

ULFHEIM (*furious then very calm*). I once took a young girl… out of the gutter. I carried her on my back. I held her tightly, next to my heart. I would have carried her all my life, protected her from all harm… clothed her in starlight… (*Weeps silently.*)

MAIA. You carried her in your arms?

ULFHEIM. And do you know how she repaid me?

MAIA. No. How?

ULFHEIM. She went back to the gutter. Left me my ugly little horns. The ones you can't see but I can feel. So now you can laugh at me.

MAIA. I'm not laughing. I have a story too.

ULFHEIM. Tell me.

MAIA. Once upon a time there was a vain little girl who was very poor. She had a loving mother and a father but she left them to run away with a rich, rich lord. He took her to all the bravest cities of the world.

ULFHEIM. Did she want to go with him?

MAIA. Oh yes. Then. She was such a fool.

ULFHEIM. Was he handsome and strong?

MAIA. No. Very ugly. But he promised to take her high into the mountains where everything was glorious light – brilliant sunshine –

ULFHEIM. I see. A mountaineer?

MAIA. In one sense.

ULFHEIM. Or a mountain goat. And did he carry her up to the mountain tops?

MAIA. He took her halfway. In fact, he took her in. Fooled her. Shut her in a cold, dark, dank room and surrounded it with evil shadows and monsters shaped in stone –

ULFHEIM. Good! It served her right.

MAIA. Yes it did. Now you can laugh at me.

ULFHEIM (*studies her*). Do you know what I'm thinking?

MAIA. No. What?

ULFHEIM. I think both our lives are worn to rags and tatters.

MAIA. I think so too.

ULFHEIM. Have we enough rags to stitch into a single life?

MAIA. What? Join them together? Rags? What happens when they fall to bits?

ULFHEIM. Then we'll both be beautiful, naked, and free at last – we'll be ourselves.

MAIA. And everybody will see your goat's legs. And laugh at them.

ULFHEIM. And everybody will see your prickly little –

MAIA. No! Come on! We've got to go.

ULFHEIM. Go where? What's the hurry?

MAIA. Down to the hotel.

ULFHEIM. There's no fun to be had there.

MAIA. None at all. So… We'll say goodbye.

ULFHEIM. I'm not sure it's that simple.

MAIA. Yes it is. You didn't manage to put me on the leash.

ULFHEIM. I could offer you a castle.

MAIA. Is it very grand? – Like that sty over there?

ULFHEIM. It's not in ruins – not quite –

MAIA. 'And all the kingdoms of the world', perhaps?

ULFHEIM. No kingdom – just a castle.

MAIA. I've had my fill of castles.

ULFHEIM. Set in a few hundred square miles of the finest hunting country –

MAIA. Is it stuffed with works of art?

ULFHEIM (*apologetically*). I'm afraid not. Art's not my line.

MAIA (*relieved*). Well, thank God for small mercies!

They both laugh harshly.

ULFHEIM. Maia? Will you come with me?

MAIA. There's an old buzzard who won't let me out of his sight.

ULFHEIM. We'll clip his wings.

MAIA. Down we go then. Help me.

A storm begins. Thunder far off.

ULFHEIM (*holding her*). Yes. We'd better hurry. There's a mist coming. Then the storm will be on us.

MAIA. Is it really as dangerous as you said?

ULFHEIM. It is. And with the mist it will soon be impossible.

She goes to the edge and looks over; she jumps back; he laughs.

It makes your head spin?

MAIA. Yes. But there's – Go and look for yourself.

He does.

ULFHEIM. They must be mad. The old buzzard and the walking corpse.

MAIA. Is there any way we can get down without them seeing us?

ULFHEIM. No. There's just that track. Only a few inches wide in places.

MAIA. Then we'll just have to stand our ground.

ULFHEIM. That's the spirit! Good boy! Good dog!

RUBEK and IRENA climb up; they are well wrapped against the cold, she in white fur and a swansdown hood.

RUBEK. Maia?

MAIA (*confident*). Come up. You've almost made it.

RUBEK helps IRENA.

RUBEK (*coldly*). Been out all night?

MAIA. Yes.

RUBEK. So have we.

MAIA. Hunting. You said I could.

ULFHEIM. You climbed up that track?

RUBEK. Obviously.

ULFHEIM. She too?

RUBEK. Obviously. There is only one track. We took it. We mean to keep on it.

ULFHEIM. You never will, though. It's crumbling away. (*Snorts in disbelief.*) I'm surprised you've got this far. You could have broken your necks.

RUBEK. Yes, easily. It wasn't so steep when we started out.

ULFHEIM. It never is, is it? But there are too many slippery ledges where you can bugger yourselves – can't go forward, can't go back.

RUBEK (*ironic smile*). Thank you for the lesson in philosophy, Baron Ulfheim.

ULFHEIM. Philosophy's not my line, Rubek. I'm worrying about survival. What were you thinking of, man? The storm's coming down. We'll be shrouded in mist any minute.

IRENA *shudders at the word 'shrouded' and repeats it silently to herself.*

Listen to it.

RUBEK. Judgement day's coming.

ULFHEIM. We'll be caught if we don't move.

MAIA. Come on then!

ULFHEIM. You two will never make it. You'd better shelter in the hut over there and I'll send somebody up to rescue you when the worst is over.

RUBEK. Do we need rescuing?

ULFHEIM. You'll never get down on your own.

IRENA (*panics*). I'm not going down. I refuse! No –

ULFHEIM. Then you'll have to be carried down. Your sort's a danger to yourselves and everybody else. People get killed up here – all the time –

MAIA. Then let's go!

ULFHEIM. Come on. I've got hold of you.

MAIA. I'll be lucky to get out of this in one piece.

ULFHEIM. Trust me. I know what I'm doing. You'd better make a dash for the hut. I'll send up some ropes.

With MAIA *holding on to him – he's almost carrying her – they climb down over the edge.*

Go on! Get to the hut!

IRENA (*stares at* RUBEK; *she's very agitated*). I won't go back down there. Ropes – force –

RUBEK. Calm down –

IRENA (*more and more agitated*). They'll bring her with them – and the straitjacket – and they'll tie me – ropes –

RUBEK. Calm down, Irena!

IRENA. She has it in the trunk – I've seen it – They'll force me to –

RUBEK. Nobody's going to force you to –

IRENA. Nobody will force me! (*Pulls out the knife.*)

RUBEK. What are you doing –

IRENA. Look. Nobody will force me –

RUBEK. Give that to me –

IRENA. No. I have to keep it close – day and night – awake or asleep –

RUBEK. Irena!

IRENA. No! I may need it. (*Hides it.*)

RUBEK. What for?

IRENA. Oho!

RUBEK. Hand it over. Come on!

IRENA (*looks at him hard*). I was going to kill you, Arnold. I've hated you so long –

RUBEK. Kill me? Is this another of your –

IRENA. Yesterday evening. Down at Lake Taunitz.

RUBEK. Lake Taunitz? But… What are you talking about?

IRENA. We were sitting outside our cottage, playing with the swans and the boats… water lilies… swans…

RUBEK. Irena. Your mind must be –

IRENA. The sun was setting… Didn't you say to me? – Oh, you were so cold… Like ice. Like death. You said that word… 'association'. You thought of me – our life – as 'an association'…

RUBEK. I never said that! Never! It's something you told yourself!

IRENA. So I took out the knife. I wanted… I wanted to drive it into the back of your neck – up into the brain.

RUBEK. Then what stopped you?

IRENA. I saw there was no longer any need, Arnold. What would be the point?

RUBEK. The point?

IRENA. In taking your life? I saw you too were already dead. Dead and cold.

RUBEK. Dead?

IRENA. A horror…

RUBEK. Dead.

IRENA. As I am. We were playing by the lake – like drowned corpses given motion only by the movement of the water.

RUBEK. It's not death, Irena. Not to me. How can I make you accept that?

IRENA. Oh, when I was young and naked… You say you were burning for me –

RUBEK. I loved you –

IRENA. You resisted that love – fought against it – struggled. You saw me as that young girl – innocence rising from the grave.

RUBEK. I loved you, Irena.

IRENA. There was a time – oh, when we burned with life. We walked on earth in the sunlight – childlike – and everything was new and wonderful and charged with mystery. That's what's dead. We can never have that back. That awakening of love. That's over. What is a life? And love… it dies so quickly.

RUBEK. I love you, Irena. I have such love.

IRENA. After what I've become?

RUBEK. You're as you always were. I've held you – in my mind – fixed you in dreams.

IRENA. Naked on a turntable – for hundreds of men since you.

RUBEK. I drove you to that. I put my art – an image of clay above a body burning with life. But I loved you, Irena.

IRENA (*drooping; laughs silently*). It's too late – we've wasted away. Life's all gone.

RUBEK. Nothing you've done – nothing you've suffered – has diminished you. In my eyes, you are innocence.

IRENA (*assertively*). And in my own.

RUBEK. Then how can it be too late? We're free to do as we please – for the rest of our lives.

IRENA (*sadly*). I've no longer the strength for life. I'm barely out of the tomb –

RUBEK. You're wrong –

IRENA. I'm used up. And you're dead – as I was. You've left me. I came too late.

RUBEK. Life renews itself – everything bursts into flower again. It's still strong in us, Irena.

IRENA. We are not flowers. (*Smiling*.) It's just words – without meaning. Feelings – our senses wear out. Youth – the passion in us won't endure… (*Bitterly*.) It's not hard like your art. But we go on and on – hoping – building vision upon youthful vision – and suddenly there's no time. It's gone – before we've even begun.

RUBEK (*laughing – he lifts her up and embraces her violently*). Well, if death's all there is – a pair of graves – let's squeeze every last drop out of what's left to us. Let's not watch ourselves slow and fade into the darkness – I'm not going without a fight!

IRENA. Arnold!

RUBEK. And I'll choose my ground! It's not going to be here in this gloom – a damp mist for a shroud –

IRENA. No – up there! We'll climb up through the mist into the light –

RUBEK. Come on then! I want to see the sun –

IRENA. I want the glory of the world! – It's what you promised – Up there, up on the mountain tops.

RUBEK. My only love.

IRENA. I want the sun. I want the sun to bathe us in light.

RUBEK. It will! I promise you – up there we'll find the glory of the world – out of the darkness into the light. (*Pulls her towards the path*.)

IRENA. Give me that and I'll fall down and worship you –

RUBEK. Up through the mist –

IRENA. Up through the mist – We'll see the sun rise on the mountain tops. And all the glory of the world.

RUBEK. Come on!

They climb up through the mist and disappear; the storm envelops everything; the NUN *climbs up, looking for* IRENA; *suddenly an avalanche hurtles down the mountain carrying* RUBEK *and* IRENA *to their deaths; the* NUN *screams over the storm, reaches out to them then crosses herself and silently mouths the words* 'pax vobiscum'.

NUN. Irena!

The End.

A Nick Hern Book

Judgement Day, adapted from *When We Dead Awaken* by Henrik Ibsen, first published in Great Britain as a paperback original in 2011 by Nick Hern Books Limited, 14 Larden Road, London W3 7ST, in association with The Print Room

Judgement Day copyright © 2011 Mike Poulton

Mike Poulton has asserted his right to be identified as the author of this version

Cover image: Veronica Humphris
Cover design: Ned Hoste, 2H

Typeset by Nick Hern Books, London
Printed in Great Britain by Mimeo Ltd, Huntingdon,
Cambridgeshire PE29 6XX

A CIP catalogue record for this book is available from the British Library

ISBN 978 1 84842 241 4

.